THE CIVILIZED
LEADER

LOUISA AKAISO

Library and Archives Canada Cataloguing in Publication

CIP data on file with the National Library and Archives

ISBN trade paperback 978-1-55483-869-1
ISBN e-book 978-1-55483-870-7

Disclaimer:

TABLE OF CONTENTS

FOREWORD

If you are like me, you probably heard the words civil and civility tossed about and did that little mental flip-flop and turned them into polite and courteous and thought "all good." If you did, guess what, you be would be wrong too.

As someone who has traveled internationally as a business and personal development trainer and coach, as well as being a member of the John C. Maxwell team, I thought I got this civil/civility thing locked down.

Man was I wrong.

I had been raised to keep my elbows off the table and taught how to avoid the use of certain words and phrases in mixed company.

So, it was easy to assume that I was a civilized leader.

What I learned quickly from Louisa Akaiso and her training was that all those behaviors were fine and good, but that was not entirely civility, I had just touched the surface of what it meant to be both civil and a leader.

You see Louisa has taken what she learned from our common mentor John C. Maxwell, *"that leadership is influence, nothing more, nothing less"* and infused her very in-depth knowledge of civility and corporate cultures and raised the bar on what is required to be a leader and introduced the next level of leadership: the civilized leader.

As a civilized leader, I now view leadership as more than just influence. I am learning, thanks to my friend Louisa, that to be a civilized leader, I must understand my leadership must comes from the perspective of treating others as *they would like to be treated*.

To treat others as they would like to be treated, I as a leader, must look at those I lead as unique individuals with their own histories, cultures and 'hot buttons.' I have to think about how my actions impact the individuals around me. Leadership cannot be a tool to push people into a direction or behavior. Civilized leadership pulls people and teams together around respect and a desire to fulfill a common goal.

It is no surprise that nearly 9 in 10 Americans who work in uncivil environments report that incivility has negative consequences on their job and at home, costing companies millions of dollars in lost productivity.

In this age of lost 'Political Correctness' we had have landed in an ethical and linguistic swamp. 'Free-Speech' or 'I'm free to say absolutely anything about anyone without any consequences' has resulted in increased workplace tension, violence and lost productivity. In this rapidly shifting corporate culture it is imperative that every leader read and study *The Civilized Leader*.

Developing a culture of civility is not a new form

of political correctness, censorship, or deception. It is about building a culture of respect, motivation, and success. It is about moving beyond management and to the next level, civilized leadership.

As someone who has studied business and leadership and has been privileged to train both highly successful teams and companies as well as spending thousands of hours coaching both entrepreneurs and executives, I can say the timing of this book and tools provided in it could not be more relevant and necessary.

My advice: take this book, read it, study it, do the homework required, and become a civilized leader.

Take your leadership to the next level.

Thank you, Louisa, for the impact and influence you have had on me.

Eric G. Reid
Found Success Life
YourSuccessLife.com

There could not have been a better person to write about civilized leadership than Louisa Akaiso. Civility is not what she does or what she teaches. Civility is who she is. I have watched Louisa consistently demonstrate the very notions and practices that she beautifully presents in this book and continue to be inspired by her authentic, caring, loving and life-giving style of leadership.

If you desire to reach your full leadership potential where you see your influence multiplied, then read this book. And if you aspire to leave a legacy of leadership that positively changes the world through excellence in civility, then I invite you to go even further and put into practice the useful knowledge that you are about to glean from this masterpiece.

Muriel Ngo Batet
Life Coach, Author and Leadership Trainer

Civility is a human need, equal to anything that humans can celebrate. In the last year, I have interviewed over a hundred middle-class people from around the world, and less than ten of them can adequately capture the most basic ideas of civility. Some studies show that incivility exists even in some of the best organizations to work for. A survey found that 98% of the workers, over a period of about 20 years, experienced rude behavior and 99% had witnessed it.

Civility is a human need with no substitute, and therefore a human right. It is one of those prerequisites to meaningful and self-actualization that you are either blessed with loads of it, or you stretch to find a means to gift yourself with it. Whichever way, it is a constant in the human life that you graciously share with others around you.

Louisa's commitment is noble, and her vision is authentic. Her book is full of useful and transferable 'how-to's' she has so practically and professionally captured. And of particular note is the clarity delivered in each chapter, the evaluation pages where knowledge learned can be tested, the fresh goals about how much needs to be done to reach desired ends, and much more.

Civility is one of our needs, and Louisa has done well in adding her mastery to the possibilities humanity can use. *The Civilized Leader* is a must-read.

Olakunle A. Soriyan (aka PK)
Winter 2018

The Objective of this Book

The civilized leader embraces the golden rule, and defines how to weave all of the leadership attributes together to influence change, and to lead with humanity and compassion. Civility and leadership are a powerful combination, so powerful that they seem like magic. What civility and leadership are, are not easy to say. However, when you see someone using them, you know that what you are looking at is something very special, and very powerful. Do you remember Admiral Horatio or Florence Nightingale? They had these gifts.

As a civility trainer and leadership expert, I am providing you with a resource toolkit to inspire you, through my course of learning, observation, and experience from practicing leaders. The resources contained in this book will make you see that you are capable of what you have always wanted to be.

Some people exhibit leadership traits. However, they do not know how to teach it to others. They might say things like, "I don't know, it just worked out." "I can't explain the principle behind this; I just know that whenever I do this, it works for me." They can't explain how or where they acquired their know-how; they only know that they have the skills and that these skills work. These people are the first to admit that they are not able to teach their skills effectively. The same goes for civility: some people seem to acquire it through a certain kind of upbringing or they are born with it. They are considerate and cheerful, and people almost inevitably respond to them enthusiastically, but they are unable to explain why they have a pleasant workplace. The necessity for broader civility is required.

The Civilized Leader is the product of many years of experience. I have studied people who have excellent leadership skills together with very civil ways of interacting with people. I have learned a great deal from them, and over the years I have figured out what they do and how they do it. And it is not just about doing, it is about acquiring a certain kind of attitude, the attitude of someone who thinks people are important and deserve our kindness and consideration.

This is not a book about arcane, mysterious principles; it is a clear book whose purpose is to teach you precisely what civility and leadership are and how, once you understand them, you can utilize them. Once you start using them, you will see amazing changes occur in the people around you. They will be impressed by who you are, will want to emulate you. They will be changing radically for the better. How great it will be for you because you will have the deep satisfaction of knowing that you have been a positive force in people's lives.

This book is not about theory. It is about practicality, and I will show you how the principles (and techniques) of leadership and civility have been used effectively in many real-life situations. When people know how to use the principles of this book they find that they are suddenly more productive, more adept at working with others, and, overall, a more positive force. If the people in an organization are taught these skills and how to utilize them, you can be sure that the productivity of that organization will increase dramatically. And the effect of all these changes, in their way, will make this world a little better place.

This book has been written to motivate you to understand how civility can improve the productivity and the atmosphere within your organization. It aims at offering recipes on how we can develop ourselves to the fullness of our capabilities and influence. It also reveals answers to many practical hurdles leaders have to overcome.

The Civilized Leader is a hands-on book: after some important discussions, there are evaluation pages where you can test yourself on what you have learned, and determine how much you need to do to reach your anticipated destination. You will also find quizzes that test your knowledge, assess your personal development and chart a course for assimilating what you have learned.

I look forward to celebrating your success at the end of this book. See you at the peak of your leadership life and expression!

Yours in greatness,
Louisa Akaiso.

INTRODUCTION

Everyone loves the united activity of an organization. By organization, I don't mean a business venture, necessarily. It could be a group of friends taking charge. It could be a number of individuals taking on communal responsibility. It could be a set of school kids, presenting a Shakespearean sonnet in a coordinated manner. In instances like this, the audience and viewers of these performances praise the team for their renditions. More, they praise the person who assumes the leading role, for the coordination.

Leadership happens amongst us, from the simplest family unit to the most complex business organizations. People attain leadership positions in four main ways:

- They are born into it.
- They grow into it, with responsibilities lying on their shoulder, which they can't run from.
- They desire it in themselves, and they become it.
- They are pushed into it.

If you consider yourself a leader or you happen to have someone whom you influence, evaluate yourself. You will realize that you fall into one of these categories.

John Maxwell, the award-winning author, explained four types of leaders in his book, *Developing the*

Leader within You.

- The leading leader is considered to be born with leadership qualities and has learned to nurture these qualities through self-discipline.
- The learned leader was not born with leadership qualities, but he learned them.
- The latent leader has recently learned leadership qualities and is building on these qualities.
- The limited leader has little or no exposure to leadership, but he desires to lead.

I have seen how men handled leadership; for some, I am impressed, for some, I am not. What gives me joy, for which I am humbled, is that I can tell by deductive reasoning, the possibility for a leadership betterment.

Also, the ability to lead does not end with knowing how to get people into (a) team(s) and drive them. There is more. The psychology of man has shown that with the elaboration of the world and its prospects, human desires and aspirations widen, and change with time. Hence, something more startling becomes a topic for consideration. "How do I lead a team of people with varying interests and propensity to change in different ways, to achieve a common goal with a common attitude?"

It is simple. You need to become a civilized leader. It could take a while to achieve this, but you will get there. One of my teachers told a story about a young boy who was the son of a carpenter. The lad would hit the hammer on a nail about ten times before the nail was driven into the wood. He would ask his father, why he wasn't able to drive the nail with three strokes as the father would. The father smiled. "When I was your age, I would probably take thirteen strokes to drive a nail in. With consistency, the hammer will trust your hand with precision, and the nail will suffer less."

Welcome to the civilized leadership awakening in you!

From the above options of how people attain leadership, list the one(s) to which you think applies to you.

_____

_____

What three things led you to such a position?

_____

_____

_____

Do you remember your first reaction in each of the situations? Write them down.

_____

_____

_____

As we go on, this will help you keep track of your attributes and how you can possibly improve on them. Also, the reflection on those moments will make it easier for you to point at the basic principles that brought you to leadership.

CHAPTER ONE

EXPLAINING A LEADER

There is a dream I want to be –
A star, shining like the glassy moon.
There is a dream I want to be –
A rain, drenching earth unto increase.
There is a dream I want to be –
A nightingale, coloring the sky with my song.
But, how do I begin my journey to the sky?
—Louisa Akaiso

Many will define a leader in various ways. Many
will successfully explain a leader by giving an
example. It will be right to say,

- A leader is one who heads a group of people.
- A leader is the face of a sect of people.
- A leader is one who drives many people to be
  productive.
- A leader is one who stands up to shoulder re-
  sponsibilities as the need arises.
- A leader is one who understands people.

All these are right; however, they are independently
non-encompassing. To precisely define a leader, we

will have to unite all these things into one definition. *"A leader is one who understands that situations arise, and the best way to change them is developing an attitude that will create corresponding action."* This attitude might change from one situation to another; however, it does not violate the essence of humanity and integrity. Moreover, this attitude is not false or faked, even though it can be flexible.

In this way, leadership means, understanding situations, one's self, and one's environment, hence, wielding influence. The influence is directed at, at least, two of these subjects. A leader, who desires or is active, must hold this influence in direct proportion to the situation at hand and to himself. It is when he has mastered this skill that he can influence himself better and disseminate the same mastery to others.

Leadership is a coordinated influence between a circumstance and a person. This is the same conclusion that the evangelist of the leadership development, John Maxwell entrusted to his readers. *"**Leadership is Influence. That's it. Nothing more; nothing less.**"*[1] He wrote.

To understand leadership, one certainly has to understand influence.

WHAT IS INFLUENCE?

Someone once told me while I was walking out from my old office, "Louisa, I love your spirit towards work. I want to be like you." I smiled and appreciated the compliment.

The other day, I was with a friend at her child's school. Her child had come second in a swimming competition. When the child who came first was interviewed, she was asked how she was able to win first place. I heard her say, "My dad's words kept ringing in my head. 'You can beat my record.' He is a pretty fast swimmer, too."

In these instances, there is a propelling force –influence. It was an observed habit in the first instance. It was a motivated voice, in the second story. Someone said we are all products of influence. I agree.

As someone in the lead, or with the desire to be, you must be conscious of how you carry yourself. You are an influencer. You can't resign yourself to be a leader. You have to take charge of things happening around you, consciously. You need to improve in your discipline for things and people. Either success or failure, every man has the power of influence, directly or indirectly.

THE ATTRIBUTES OF A LEADER

There are certain traits found in every leader. Those traits can be either recessive, as a potential or dominant, or in plain view. These qualities can be learned, developed, and made effective by usage. One must actively understand this. **A leader must Understand Situations and Circumstance.**

In every place and instance where we have ever had someone marked out as a leader, one thing is always the same; there is a situation at hand. Someone with a shoulder, bearing a team or a group of people is a discoverer. Usually, they leave the realm of discovery into identifying how it influences people, and they raise their voice on behalf of others of their kinds.

A leader is reflective, thoughtful, and insightful about instances and their consequences (either currently or speculatively). They see a need to render a service for the people.

The voices that gained independence from oppressive forces, including the likes of Ernesto Che Guevara of Cuba, Nelson Mandela of South Africa, Mahatma Gandhi of India and many more revolutionaries understand these things. They were thoughtful and strategic.

Humanity is the greatest substance that exists. It has the most significant impact of influence. Hence, one is only considered a leader, when it has to do with the values of men. You can't hold yourself up as a leader without people.

Don't misunderstand me. I am not saying that you look for people to exert authority and influence over. Usually, your understanding and your shared ideas are what attract people to you. In the world of leadership, like attracts like. And, the orientation of the 'unlikely' can be changed to become a 'likely,' in an attractive way.

At the start, good leaders do not consider the "leadership" responsibility before they assume this mantle. They are fueled by passion and empathy.

This is what every market strategist and businessperson realizes before s/he decides to build an organization of people that would meet a specific communal need for human benefits.

A LEADER MUST BE INVOLVED IN THE GAME

One of the truest statements is, "lead by example." I cannot imagine myself a leader while I give directions to people, but I am not involved. That would mean I am an instructor, not a leader.

In the military, there are those assigned to be unit leaders. In the army, the strongest bond is between the soldiers and his unit. They believe that bond as strong or stronger than family bonds, and the leader, the head.

I remember John Maxwell said, "the boss says go; the leader says let's go!" [2] How true! Apart from the fact that people appreciate and love a leader that gets into the game, a leader will be untrue to his call by sitting behind a desk while he gets others to work towards a specific goal.

As a leader, if you intend to run for a course or incorporate a policy, you are to take the diligence to learn the science and the art of that stuff. Get your head into it. This way, you can steer the people around you to follow the same course.

I remember an old movie. It was of Chinese origin. There was a young man who came to learn martial arts in a school with other students. He was the best among them, with his skills and abilities getting sharper and better by the day. One day, while the *sensei* instructed him, he was not pleased. He said all the master could do was instruct, and he was never able to fight. He claimed to be better than the master, and that was why the *sensei* was so harsh. A sparring match was set up between this fellow and the *sensei*. As fast as the lad was, brief moves from the master cut short his attacks. Eventually, the student left the match with his tail between his legs. You see, even if a leader were to share instructions, it is better shared when he has the experience.

Just like anyone would rightly defines a leader as one with responsibilities, a leader must realize that getting into the game is part of the responsibilities.

How do you get into the game? Do you have to bother yourself with accounting, as an English major? Or do you have to immerse yourself in quantum physics, as a life scientist? It is, in fact, more straight-forward. All you need to do is to let the people in those areas of specialty know that you care so much about what they do and you honor them for their con-tributions. You, checking up on them while you are active with other things shows that you are a part of what they do. That is the place of being civil. I will ex-plain this more as we go along.

A LEADER MUST BE CAREFUL ABOUT INFLUENCE

After I have had people talk to me about how much I motivate them, and how they would love to be like me, I shared my concern about being more conscious with what I do with my husband. He wrote me what he called 'a dusty poem.' However, the poem is invaluable!

I choose to wash my legs and watch my step.
I will watch my ways and make it straight.
There is a man down the road,
Who longs to have his legs like mine.
There is a young boy in my streets;
He has molded his dreams in my shape.
I am a light that calls people to its stead
I can't afford to be dull at that which I am praised.
—Dr. Darlington Akaiso

I have this poem tucked in a dear book gifted to me by my husband, when we were newly married. Because I frequently open the book for memories and admiration, I encounter the poem often. I get vitalized even more.

As a leader, you need to understand that one of the attitudes you have to develop, is how you hold yourself (self-control). Advertently, or not, you are an influencer. For the enhancement of humanity and course that you have sworn to, you have to adapt yourself to the course you have chosen. You have to make the consciousness of influence mold your attitude about how you do the things you do. You can't fake this. It has to be adopted, to be an integral part of you.

Building influence has its costs, but it is worth it.

My birthday is a reflective event for me. I appreciate the birthday wishes I receive from people. While I am usually overwhelmed by the love, I pay more attention to people's testimonies of me and their wishes for me.

During my most recent birthday, I learned some things that I would like to share.

1. Influence stretches beyond direct contact. It reaches third parties.
2. News travels farther than a person ever would.
3. While honor comes from friend, family, members of the same faith, the weightier honor comes from people who believe in what you stand for.
4. Influence is cumulative; it is not built in a day, sometimes, not even in a year.
5. People study you, more than you relate to them.

When these things dawned on me, I braced myself. I promised people around me that I would be committed more and be conscious of my ways.

Before you were in a leadership position, you were in a position of influence with your friends, neighbors, families, and colleagues. How much more would you be, when you are called to become a leader?

Always remember, your actions are someone else's legacy.

EVALUATION

What have people publicly admired about you?

1. _____
2. _____
3. _____

What have you been told, more than once, that you needed to improve on?

1. _____
2. _____
3. _____

When was the last time you evaluated yourself?

_____

I am sure that the answers to the first question are your strong points. You should be proud of them.

The second question might make you feel uneasy. You may have believed that, when you were told, this was not true. However, if more than one person has said this, it is worth it that you check what is happening. And that leads us to the third question:

When was the last time you evaluated yourself in line with your objectives? If this is not something you do, at least, once a week, you are not faring so well. As a leader, you must never take your mind off of your objectives.

Frequently, in the South Korean's martial art, taekwondo, the students are told to recite the tenets of the art. This way, the students remind themselves why they were admitted into the classes.

I am sure that you have noticed when you enter an office, sometimes the company's objectives, missions, and visions printed on the walls. They remind the staff, as much as anyone who walks into that space, that there is a reason why they do the things they do. Whatever they have written on the wall, and obvious places tell them what they are working towards.

A LEADER SHOULD BE CIVILIZED

By civility, I mean the dictionary meaning of being reasonable, considerate, moral, and having developed societal virtues. Civility like influence must be developed and adopted. It is a virtue that goes beyond the leader.

Civility, frequently, separates a leader from a boss. While a boss cares about getting a task done, a goal met, and a target arrived at; a leader employs a more effort to provide the motivation that will get people to reach the target.

A leader cares about the motivation that produces the result. It is what shows him as humane. I will never forget one of the lessons I learned during my early times in Africa. There was an estate manager I worked for, who served a rich man. All the man ever wanted was that everywhere was clean–the fence, white; the floor, shiny; the windowpanes, spotless; and the white curtains, sparkling! He would yell if he were dissatisfied with anything in the house. However, the estate manager never related to us that way. Later the man was replaced with a woman. She would tell us stories with interesting moral lessons about why we should work. She would promise us bonuses if we were able to finish early. She would relieve a weak fellow of duty, not minding if she spent extra hours on duty. That is an attribute of a civilized leader–understanding.

Lewena Bayer in her book, *The 30% Solution*, explained how civility could increase an organization's revenue by up to 30 percent. She wrote that civility transcends being customer conscious via niceness and other 'customer-capturing' policies; it includes dealing with situations and building a process for continuous learning. She said the meaning even goes deeper into relationships with others.

From scrutiny and years of studying, I will categorize civility into two main categories

1. Understanding the ultimate resource–people.
2. Showing affection and extended relationships beyond formality.

1. UNDERSTANDING THE ULTIMATE RESOURCE – PEOPLE.

You see, as mentioned earlier, the psychology of man changes with time. Manufacturers with a customer-end line will tell you: the marketing strategies used today are not what was used five years ago. The ones used five years ago are nothing compared to the marketing model constructed a decade ago. People change. As the world evolves and civilization claims the globe, humans' desires and aspirations grow proportionately. Not just as customers, but as individuals.

When someone is coming to work with you, he has most probably seen a future of himself in your company. Hence, he also wants to be understood why he is investing his passions in your course.

In the section, "people's development," in *Developing the Leader within You*, John Maxwell spells out the fact that "people are the most valuable assets."

While dealing with people, as a leader, you need to show a great deal of understanding. Many organizations that have lost valuable people who were able to make their business flourish, owing to the lack of understanding. There was (I don't know if it still exists) a cocoa contractor for Nestle, in Nigeria. A young man was their procurement manager. The man was diligent. He knew how to speak with suppliers, so that they could keep supplying the company, steadily, even when the company was not very rich to pay immediately. The young man would make fair deals with the suppliers and talk to the director about the deals. He would tell the director how such faithful customers should be encouraged with fair prices.

The manager thought the young man was always incurring debt, even though the accounts showed the company was making a profit. In a time when the cocoa market crashed globally, this young chap was among the people that the director retrenched. That was where the law of diminishing returns began with the company.

The young man? Oh, he still knew his onions. Eventually, he struck deals with another company and the old suppliers. The last I heard of him, he was doing well, and had become a major cocoa dealer himself.

When things are not going too well, as a leader, you must never take your attention off the people. They are your ultimate resource. Building the empire, you are today, which was once a dream was because you had them. Even when market and societal values seem to be crushing your organization, don't forget to appreciate and honor these people.

Sometimes, when you pitch your ideas to people, perhaps friends, they see more hope in what you have shared than what they are currently working on. Hence, they drop their dreams for yours. In a world where uncertainty is rising, people easily dump their dreams for something they see to be more hopeful. However, they should not be taunted or spoken down to, because they have committed themselves to your league. You should appreciate the fact that people sacrifice their hopes for yours. Even if they don't say it, they want to be appreciated.

When I was ten, I found my mom cooking; she wanted to make pottage for dinner. I told her I could do it better. She asked how I knew I could. I told her I had seen her do it many times. Plus, I had magical hands when it came to cooking. She chuckled and allowed me. I fumbled. The meal in the pot looked nothing like pottage. My mom appreciated me. She encouraged me to take responsibility. As the cook, I coughed more than once, while munching the food. But my mom? I remember the look on her face. It was gracious and filled with smiles as she scooped each spoon.

As a leader, you have to value every effort and idea. Even when they go sour or do not merit action, appreciate them. Then, you can go ahead to pitch a new idea about the way forward.

Leadership is a temperament on its own. Other temperaments have to bow to it. You have to be patient with your team. Put yourself in their positions.

You need to understand their plights, the conditions under which they work, the circumstances heralding their actions and inactions. If it is something manageable, encourage them to do more. Remember, as a leader, and you must be in the game. Showing understanding is a way to put yourself in the game.

2. SHOWING AFFECTION AND EXTENDED RELATIONSHIP BEYOND FORMALITY.

Being fond of sushi, I go to a lot of places to try out the local sushi restaurants. This is a common attitude when I am in a new town, and I know that I would be staying for a while. I will need to get somewhere trustworthy enough for consistent patronage. There was a place in London that stood out. Although the owner of the restaurant was old, he knew the name of every member of his staff, even though they worked in shifts. Not just that, he knew the name of the regulars, as well. Before I left London, I was an acquaintance of his. I asked how he got to know his staff by their names. He replied, "I don't just know them by their names, I know their surnames."

"You see," he said, "I have realized that the way to make work enjoyable is to make them feel they matter. Hence, I get to know these folks by their names. Whenever I forget a new chap's name, I would check the register. Then I will make jokes, addressing him by his name, to make it stick in my mind. Finding a means to survive around here can be pretty tough. I don't intend to make it any tougher."

How thoughtful! During one of my conversations with the man, on a late night, I passed a comment. "A delicate food like sushi needs delicate hands, for perfection. Yours are such beautiful hands."

"Thank you, Louisa" He responded. "You know, it is easy to lose customers, once the taste changes. This kitchen is all I have left. I would do anything to preserve the integrity. 'Anything' includes making my staff feel important, giving them relief whenever they want it. It makes them committed to the cooking. A sense of importance will not let them cook the food 'anyhow,' even when I am not supervising. My mother taught me this." For many days and weeks, those words kept ringing in my head.

As a leader, you need to make your team feel important. Let every individual you can reach know that you care. Build a relationship. Build trust. Motivate them. Ask about their welfare. Show genuine affection beyond work. Affection is the heart of a leader. Adopt it. A leader must show he cares about people.

It is not weakness to show affection. I once had an encounter with a woman, a store owner that said about her best staff, "Even though I care much about her and I would be deeply worried if she leaves town, I can't afford to show it. I would be known to have a soft spot."

Really? Should what people think of you douse your fire of humanity? No. What you think people will think of you should not take away your humanity.

Bear this in mind; a civilized leader is one that is regarded as humane. Leadership gets work done, conveniently and efficiently, more than bossiness does. Even though you can get a result by being bossy, try being a leader. You will realize results can be achieved with much less effort.

Civility is an attitude you must train yourself to develop, as a leader. Humanity is the greatest characteristic a human can display.

EVALUATION

1. What will be my first reaction if I realize a staff member was absent from duty?
2. What will be my first reaction if a staff member was late for work?
3. When last did someone say to me, "thank you for checking on me"?
4. Has anyone ever told me that inquisitiveness about their/someone else's welfare is a weakness?
5. "The open display of care is a weakness."

    a) Have I ever thought of this?

    b) Did I think about that because I am careful of myself?

    c) What do I have to prove the point, inducted hearsay or personal experience?

        i. If a personal experience, how many have I had?

        ii. Is it enough to make a part make up for the whole of humanity?

You do not have to provide the answers here, necessarily. Those questions aim to direct your thought towards how you have been managing the best resource a person can ever have. Evaluate your relationship with people and consider the possibility of improving productivity. Check if the relationship between you and your staff is like buddies, rather than the stern 'boss and the junior/employee'.

    I am sure that when you have considered these

questions yourself and you will know where you stand. You will also understand how you need to drive energy into the right direction of your desire– ultimate leadership.

CHAPTER TWO

THE LEADER AND
HIS INTEGRITY

Integrity is a part of the leader's attitude. I know that you, as well as I, have heard many sermons about integrity. You understand how important it is. Because of how the world seems to be unfair sometimes, you would have thought about doing something else that neglects integrity. I have been there, too.

Integrity should be your number one principle. If you have a list with qualities that define you and you look forward to perfecting yourself, integrity should lead that list.

I would like you to understand when considering civility, whatever you plan for or do, goes beyond yourself. As a civilized leader, you are the people's person. Moreover, because you can't be called the people's person without the people, you have to adopt anything that would make you true; to yourself and the people.

A leader must be flexible in his prospects, with time, people, and his reactions to situations. However, his integrity must not be compromised by fluidity.

WHY INTEGRITY?

Just like influence, integrity transcends you, the leader. What is kind of organization has aspirations but no integrity? It is like cloth, starched and ironed well, put on display for sale. However, with a little wetness from the rain, even if the sun comes back on, the glory of its straightness is gone.

In the book, *Objections Answered*, R. C. Sproul writes about Karl Marx, the founder of the communism. Karl was fond of his father. He always admired the way the man composed himself piously in the synagogue. A situation arose, and they had to move to another town.

There was no synagogue in this new town. The only church in the town was Lutheran. This church had most of the people of the community in attendance, great people of influence and affluence. To the family's shock, his father declared they would have to abandon the Jewish faith and become Lutherans. The family inquired what brought about the decision. The father simply replied, "It will be good for business." And that was it. That was what created bitterness in young Karl. That was what made him tag religion as "opiate for the masses."

Do you know the number of communists that there are in the world today? Do you know the number of followers Karl was able to gather? That is because a man–the father compromised his integrity to his faith because of money.

As I had said earlier, integrity transcends one's self.

Integrity molds two things
1. Influence
2. Reputation

1. INFLUENCE

Consider Karl Marx's story. The young man, in every sense, adored the integrity of his family's Jewish worship. He valued the zeal he saw in his father. It is most probable that he already had the aspirations to be like the man. Then, the conflict.

Integrity is what some of those that look up to you would pick up from you. I have met with sweet children who would say, "I can't do that." When you ask them why not, they reply, "My daddy told me it is not good." There, you have the fusion of integrity with influence. It is much easier to be studied than 'to be.' That is why you must have invested in yourself before you latch on to the position of leadership. Investing values require time.

It is true there are things that you learn 'on the go.' However, a virtue like integrity should have been molded from the base. If you are already in the position, and you want to develop yourself, then you have to invest it in the most conscious state with dedicated time.

THE INTEGRITY METER:

Here is something I designed for myself. I call it the Relationship Integrity Meter. Periodically, I evaluate myself with it. You should also try it out. As you regularly make strides to be better about your integrity status, come back and test yourself, to measure your development.

Here is what to do. Get a sheet of paper and record the number in front of your answer. If the answer to question A, for you, is '2', write '2' on the sheet of paper.

A. Have I ever told anyone how I feel?
1. Yes
2. Not exactly
3. No
4. There is no way on earth I can ever tell anyone

B. Have I been sincere to myself?
1. Yes
2. I think I am
3. No.
4. I am too afraid to bring myself to that reality.

C. Why do I hate the things I hate?
1. I don't like them.
2. I think I am just being indifferent about them.
3. I find them repulsive.
4. They remind me of my inabilities.

D. Why am I doing what I do?
1. It is my passion.

2. It is what is trendy and available.
3. I am doing it because it works.
4. Because I see people who are willing to go for it.

E. Why am I nice to a particular fellow?
   1. I simply love her.
   2. I don't know. I guess she is just lovable.
   3. There is something I will like to get from her.
   4. Sincerely, I think it is hypocrisy.

Add up the numbers you have there. Here is a psychological analysis of your result. You should understand that this result is not final. It is only an evaluating system to enhance your leadership integrity. No matter what the outcome is, there is always the chance for improvement.

Moreover, since you have sincerely answered the questions, it does not mean you are untrue or void of total integrity. It only signifies that there is something more to be added to your leadership curriculum vitae.

16-20:
- You are direct with principles and firm; it is a good thing for a leader. However, you need to learn to be more flexible and accommodating when dealing with people.
- You should not quiet the humanity in you; it is integral to you. We were human first before we

came together to achieve a common goal.

13-15

- You have in-depth knowledge about things.
- You are undoubtedly principled.
- You are gifted with the ability to think.
- You still need to work on your sincerity when dealing with people.

9-12:

- You have a charitable heart that can still be maximized.
- You must stand up to be intentional about your choices and actions.
- Be true to yourself.
- As a leader, you must consciously form your intention and mature them into your unconsciousness.

5-8:

- You have made yourself up to a reputable standard.
- You have an open heart, and you are a person of the people.
- Do not relax; there is always room for improvement.

An influence that is conceivable from your integrity is what people brand as your "value."

2. REPUTATION

The other thing that integrity linked to is reputation. Your integrity, either good or bad, becomes your reputation—people's impression of you.

Reputation becomes what someone can say about you, hence, it builds trust and credibility. If you are principled with integrity, in your personal choices of life and in dealing with people, you have formed a trust for people to earn.

This 'reputation become trust' is why people dig into the past of politicians. They check their activities in the past; they go to establish people's testimonies of each aspirant, so they can know if they can commit their lives and future into their hands. The most sought after virtue by the masses, in politics, is integrity. People want someone they can trust.

If you are aspiring to an office, political or not, you would be surprised, how far people can go in the quest of your history. Reputation is not falsehood. You cannot fake integrity; people get to know your true qualities before your leadership tenure lapses.

When people have seen your integrity, it becomes their branding tool for your reputation. For your reputation, they offer their trust to you. As a leader with integrity, you have to value the people's faith in you. You must hold your integrity, as well as their trust, in high esteem.

Credibility with the people goes beyond being clever. Cleverness can be craftiness; however, integrity holds cleverness from crossing that boundary. Hence, the credibility virtue. People are willing to sacrifice their time, places, and assets for your course. One thing they look for, always, is if you are credible.

"Why should I work on my integrity?" If you still have this question on your mind by now, I implore you to go back to read this chapter from the beginning, again. Integrity is the base of people's reputation about you and credibility with you.

Over the years, as I have shared this truth, I have two recurring questions that I would love to address in this book.

DIPLOMACY VERSUS CREDIBILITY

"You have told us about the line between credibility, cleverness, and craftiness," a young man asked me some time ago in Florida, "what is the place of diplomacy and integrity?"

It understandable that we have to be diplomatic sometimes, especially when dealing with people who are not our acquaintances. Diplomacy is not a crime. It is a courteous way of dodging things without being offensive. However, in your dealings with the people you lead, there is no reason to hide anything communal. If there is something that affects all or the organization, then you should get to tell your people; if not all, tell those who hold important positions. Diplomacy isn't lying, neither is it keeping a truth locked away to yourself. As a leader, you can't be selfish with organizational truths. There are always people to support you, whom you also consider an executive or board members; discuss with them.

As a leader, you will have to make tough decisions, but you are to make them with care. Moreover, in an organization, decision-making is not a one-person job. It is usually a unanimous say after contemplation. In moments when tough decisions are made, diplomacy comes into place with the presentation. You have to present your decisions in the most humane possible form that you can.

During the North Korea famine in 1994, a Japanese family who managed to have a sushi kitchen in the northern part of the province was affected. When the principal of the kitchen was going to lay off the staff in '95, he told them, "'I am very sorry. I wish we didn't have to do this, but you see, no one is safe. The people are our wealth. Why do we exist if those we care about the most–our customers are not well? But most of all, I am concerned about you, my staff who have become family. By next year, when this is over, I will look for you and bring us back to continue what we are doing.' Sadly, the famine lasted for another five years. But that man taught me the most about building a business." Over a decade later in Florida, a restaurant owner shared this story with me.

You see, diplomacy refers to handling matters with wisdom. As the people's leader, you are not just clever about it; you are so much into your words with every pint of humanity emanating from you. Therefore, yes, diplomacy can be found with a leader. For a leader, it comes from credibility, not cunningness.

CAN'T I JUST BE ME?

That was the question a young lady asked me after I had taken a leadership class with a group of teenage girls. Though I had given her a mild and a short answer, I went back home to think on it for days. Over the years of discussing leadership with people, the question, *"Do I have to compromise myself for others just because I want to lead them?"* comes up from time to time.

It is understandable that we differ in different ways, as much as we excel in different things. Nevertheless, if there is no reason to unite or have the same orientation about greatness, then there is no need for the seminars, workshops and other meetings that we attend. If we don't want to excel at mutual things, people won't go to churches to sit and learn about how to conform to Christ.

Just as I have mentioned earlier, leadership is a temperament of its own. If you desire the characteristics, you have to adopt its traits. The moment you are considering leadership, it is not "myself" anymore. It is "the people, which I am part of." Leadership is a responsibility for the people, not for yourself. Hence, you have to understand that you need to develop attitudes and virtues that crown you as the people's person. That is where civility comes in. The fact that different people come together to attain a certain 'culture' proves that leadership is a tribe of its own that people are born into, or they enter into.

Leadership does not take away your personality.

Instead, it enhances it. If you consider the leadership development as a hoax or something you would have to fake, then you will be too bothered about 'not losing myself.' Some people are afraid to change for the better. Are you one of them? If yes, you are not open to being a leader yet, sadly.

You do not have to give up on attaining leadership. You are the reason why this book becomes valuable. Consider the assessment shared earlier, again, on the Relationship Integrity Test. Then you need to understand the concept of change. In the next chapters, we shall consider *"your civility as a leader"* and *"integrating change."*

In conclusion, leadership does not rob you of your being. You are human first before responsibilities came by. Leadership only enhances your being, making your shoulders broad for responsibilities. The value it develops in you is what people come to appreciate as your integrity. Consequentially, that integrity is what sells you as a respectable person.

SELF-DISCIPLINE

"The choice of achieving what you want by doing things you don't want to do—self-discipline."
–John Maxwell

Everyone faces personal challenges on the path of personal development. And you have to prevail in these battles to become the person you want to be and show people you can lead. For instance, in campaigns about the women revolution, I have had to stand up on various platforms where criticisms from men came like bullets. I had sought comfort in thinking of replying the insults. I usually find the courage to shrug off the insults and present feasible and logical points to back up my position. There are times when I think it was a privilege to speak before international audiences, but I have had to battle negative thoughts very often. Eventually, I mustered the courage to move ahead and deliver the things that were expected of me.

It is easy to instruct others and to tell them what you want from them, but it is challenging to cultivate discipline for one's self. Self-discipline is a paradoxically simple but complex phenomenon. In simple terms, self-discipline is the effort that a person takes to set herself/himself a boundary within which s/he operates. In a practical terms, I define self-discipline as a conscious discipline that denies what I have always learned, so I can take up what is the ideal thing to do.

It takes conscious efforts to develop certain attitudes for a leader. Many of your attitudes were formed in your childhood. For instance, if a child grows up in a neighborhood whose language is violence, it would require rehabilitation to have that language and those ways removed from him. This is how difficult it can be for a human to unlearn old things and attributes to adopt new ones.

Nevertheless, a leader must use self-discipline to develop herself/himself. You have to develop yourself in what you want to instill in others. Discipline is what it takes to adopt the things you would need to be effective in what you do so that you can have what you desired, which negates what you have always known. One who has succeeded in this attitude has passed the first requirement for a leader.

On my dressing mirror, I had this statement pasted, "If I can conquer myself, I can conquer anything." I came from the past into the present upon this bridge. It also reminded me of what I am capable of and what I needed to get under control to achieve what I want. I am the aura that follows my personality. We are the shadow that follows our bodies.

Working on one's self is a life-long project. Therefore, one must not be too lazy to start the job. The earlier, the better. So, how do I get to work on myself to achieve the things that I want to achieve?

- Set your goals
- Fit the goals into milestones with time frames
- Evaluate yourself with questions and meditations
- Acknowledge your success on each point and move on to the next
- Develop a personal technique with which you can achieve what you want to achieve
- Get people that can help

SET YOUR GOALS

Once you realize the things you would love to achieve, the first thing is to list them down. Write down what you have seen in people which you desire to adopt for yourself as qualitiies.

I prefer to have a different book or diary to write these things down in. The points would be developed later and occasionally referred to. Therefore, it is better to have it in a separate book for them. When you have set these goals, own them. Be determined to get them. That is why it is self-discipline.

FIT THE GOALS INTO MILESTONES AND TIMEFRAMES.

When you have set the goals, under each one, put the number of days or months it will take you to achieve them. Set realistic times. Think about how much it would take. Searching the internet, reading books, or journals about these goals will help you determine how long it will take you to achieve them.

GOAL AT A GO

Take one goal at a time. Don't be too anxious to achieve everything at once. Virtues are developed over a lifetime. Be patient. Be realistic with your goals. Every thousand mile journey begins by putting one foot in front of the other. You might have to set a scale of preference for your goals. You will choose the ones that you think matter the most at a particular time. Go in the order that you think is best for you.

EVALUATE YOURSELF

With each goal at hand, you should evaluate yourself to make sure you are meeting your goals. During the period of evaluation, you will have to go through meditations. Be meditative and reflective.

ACKNOWLEDGE YOUR SUCCESSES

It is an ideal thing to celebrate your success. For every milestone of a goal achieved, be grateful. Appreciate your progress. Just like a child learning to walk is cheered after each step, cheer yourself. If you walk today, places you crawled yesterday, you will be able to run tomorrow. Self-appreciation is energetic. Embrace it.

DEVELOP A PERSONAL TECHNIQUE WITH WHICH YOU CAN ACHIEVE WHAT YOU WANT

For each of your goals, there might be many ways to go about achieving them. In your process of study and research, you might come to understand the diverse ways. However, just one thing might work for you. You are to experiment with many things before you decide which works best for you. For example, if you need to wake up early, you could try setting an alarm. You could try to set multiple alarms on your phone, in case one alert might not be enough. You could place your alarm some distance away from your bed so that you can get to work. You could get a friend to call you on Skype. You could have your housemate or spouse wake you up. You might have to try a number of them before you get one that works for you. The fact that you are not making progress using one technique does not mean you have failed, or that you cannot achieve it. Self-discipline is work.

GET PEOPLE THAT CAN HELP

Something that I have realized works effectively in goal realizations is when people have someone whom they are accountable to. There are times when we do not have enough motivation to carry out some tasks on our own. There are moments when discouragement or frustration can hold one down. Hence, having someone who you can talk to about your goals help. It is helpful to have someone whom you admire help you achieve your goals. It drives you to do more. When you know the person would ask questions about your progress, and you don't want to disappoint, you are geared to fuel up your pursuit. You could have mentors, or you can have a therapist on delicate matters such as anger management.

It is possible to realize that a goal is taking longer than you had expected it would. Don't slack off. So far you know you are making progress, do not relent. Actually, in your book containing your personal goals, you could give yourself an extended time or instances where you might not be able to have a precise date when this goal will be achieved.

Self-control determines your fitness. It is an act of being true to yourself. It forms and builds the core of your integrity because it begins with you. If you can tame yourself, changing the world only becomes easier. It is the attitude that defines a leader's confidence and composure. Go for it!

"I am not afraid of storms, for I am learning to sail my ship."–**Aeschylus**.

You can assess yourself on each goal.

Personal Goal Development

- Is there a noticeable change?
- Has anyone made a comment about the new attitude?
- Am I honest with myself while working on my goals?
- Am I doing this because I want to trigger emotions or because I want to develop my character?
- What was the last mistake I did about this thing today, or recently? Will I be able to handle it better now?

CHAPTER THREE

YOUR CIVILITY AS A LEADER

WHAT IS CIVILITY?

There are many definitions of civility, they only vary by a little degree, but there is a central idea that binds all these definitions. Here are some dictionary definitions of in the word.

Wikipedia

* Civility comes from the word *civilis*, which in Latin means "citizen." Civility is more than the individual's actions as a citizen. When civility functions properly usually many citizens are performing their civic duties by taking part in the political process (voting, governance), which is also known as civic engagement.[1]

Merriam Webster Dictionary

* civilized conduct; especially: courtesy, politeness
* polite act or expression[2]

Merriam Webster Thesaurus

* act or utterance that is a customary show of good manners[3]

Civility Experts Inc.

- conscious awareness of the impact of one's thoughts, actions, words and intentions on others; combined with,
- continuous acknowledgment of one's responsibility to ease the experience of others (e.g., through restraint, kindness, non-judgment, respect, and courtesy); and,
- consistent effort to adopt and exhibit civil behavior as a non-negotiable point of one's character.[4]

The act of courtesy and politeness connect all these definitions. Note: it is not something hidden away, and you have to act it out.

Civility is an integral part of leadership. It distinguishes a leader from a boss or a general. It is an established cordiality between the leader and the people. I have pointed at bits and pieces from this chapter, to show the attributes and values of a leader as the people's person.

In America, it is not uncommon to see incivility in the workplace. I have had my share of such acts, as a staff member and a customer. Many establishments and business owners get into the game of productivity. From interactions, interviews, and observations I have come to realize that most business owners are after profits solely. The majority of them do not care about what they trample on, so far it is not the law.

According to the poll conducted by the *Harvard Business Review*, over a period of 14 years, it has been reported that 98 percent of the workers in the US and Canada have been subjected to uncivil treatments [5]. There are many repercussions to this, like the reputation of a business, the owner, and the productivity of such organizations.

Incivility has many forms. They can be abuses, yells, disrespect, teases, unfavorable working conditions, and lots more. When I think of situations like this, I feel sober, and I sit down to reevaluate my prospects:

* Why do I want to lead?
* Am I getting the intended results I had before taking up this responsibility?
* Why am I gathering the people around me?
* Am I leading a dictatorship?
* If this were to be a business enterprise, will I be profitable, as I ought to?
* If I am the voice of the people, do the people like the sound they hear?

You see, to have profit as your only goal you cannot become a wholesome leader. This is because; you would be driven by everything possible to make sure you are making a profit. Making a profit is not bad. It is needed because that is why 'for profit' enterprises exist. However, with that single goal, the best thing a man can ever get is wealth, which turns out to be selfish. Check anywhere, a company with an apparent quest for profit does not have a civilized leader.

Repeatedly, while in the spa, I have heard ladies call their bosses "selfish bastard." Though abusive, they have a similar canvas on which they paint their bosses–selfishness.

For a leader who is concerned about productivity either by revenue or by visible results, civility is the way forward. In psychology, productivity and efficiency are mutually birthed when people work in a relaxed and comfortable situation. Talking about quality and perfection, a group of people working under duress would only give an estimated result per time, if compared to another group that works with the same resources under a relaxed atmosphere. The latter is more prone to meeting and exceeding the target with the utmost utilization of the resources available, than the former.

It is the way emotions work. For example, if you know people who work in a bank, they can make use of several sheets of paper in a day. For every new cash entry and summary, it is possible that the responsible staff take a fresh paper. They do so with the mentality, "We make money for the bank, we will also spend it, as much as we can."

Having another set of staff to whom civility is extended, they would be mindful about wasting resources. A thought like this guides their action, "We are trying to make a profit. More can be achieved if the bank's resources are economically utilized." Wastage and excesses are minimized in the community with a civilized working environment. Unlike an uncivil workplace.

As a leader, if you deploy civility, you are prone to being more effective.

According to the report gathered by the *Harvard Business Review*[5], while analyzing the cost of incivility, polling 800 managers and employees within 17 industries the following was reported:

- 48% intentionally decreased their work effort.
- 47% intentionally decreased the time spent at work.
- 38% intentionally decreased the quality of their work.
- 80% lost work time worrying about the incident.
- 63% lost work time avoiding the offender.
- 66% said that their performance declined.
- 78% said that their commitment to the organization declined.
- 12% said that they left their job because of the uncivil treatment.
- 25% admitted to taking their frustration out on customers.

I ask people I meet, who care about leadership: "*Do you want to raise a people for the purpose of production, or do you want to raise people that would be productive on the platform of relationship?*" There is a difference between the two. Bossiness is the first. Leadership is the latter.

Every organization, either profit oriented or not,

is concerned about productivity. For this reason, would you not rather work for a company that is solely concerned with profits or one that is also concerned about the well-being of its employees?

Let me share with you, here is what happens when a leader is void of civility,

- The people's voices and ideas are suppressed
- Team spirit deteriorates
- Customers feel the impact of such an attitude, and they leave
- The cost of input to get the desired output rises.

1. SUPPRESSED VOICES AND IDEAS

When people work in an uncivil office, their opinions don't count for much. Many of the staff would prefer to be silent. Something that matters in a producer-consumer link organization is that the staff is the best face of the office that mingles with the crowd. That way, they examine the competitors that are in the market. However, once the members of the organization feel they have no voice, they keep mute about what they hear.

Creativity in a dictatorship organization is silenced.

2. TEAM SPIRIT DEGRADATION

In an uncivil workplace, tension builds up not only between the boss and the employees, and it builds up between the workers. The tension leads to abuses, grudges and sometimes, fistfights among workers. Why? Because they can't help it, they project their aggression and frustration onto each other.

As an undergraduate, a lecturer shared a story about how humans use attitudes to find stability for themselves. Although funny, I have taken the time to study my actions and some random persons' sometimes. And, guess what? I found out it is true!

While rushing to class, as a student, you made your way around things and people; jumping and bumping into them. You would get to the class and sit down. Sometimes, you just talked to your friend sitting beside you. Sometimes, when tensed, you paced up and down, trying to become calm. When annoyed, you talked to yourself, calming yourself.

This same principle is what I have found applicable when people transfer aggression or kindness to others. For aggression, often they can't help it. It comes as an outburst regardless of surroundings.

Once people exchange angry words team spirit diminishes. It creates sects within an organization.

3. CUSTOMERS GET AFFECTED

As explained in the point above, customers also feel the impact of the tension of incivility. This impact can be either observed directly through verbal or body language from an attendant or indirectly by the strict-moodiness of the service area.

The result? The customer base and patronage are affected. You will agree with me, no one enjoys a service offered with tension.

4. THE INPUT-TO-OUTPUT RESOURCES BECOME EXPENSIVE.

Irritation among staff would cause them to mis-manage resources. Sometimes, they waste it; other times, they squander it. Irritation aside, observations have yielded results, when people work under tension, they are more subjected to breakages and mishandling of resources from fumbling. No matter what these employees do, once it affects something that is meant to contribute to the output, it becomes the responsibility of the boss or the management of the organization to get a replacement.

Also, the (work) time meant to be used to generate an estimated amount of yield becomes wasted in quarreling. Yes, time is also a factor of production. Sadly, unlike money or other resources, once lost, it cannot be retrieved.

The Harvard Business Review[5] gave the instance of an organization that had to bring in lawyers to solve the lack civility among their staff. The cost of restoring peace to the organization scales up, throughout the year. This includes 13 percent of their annual working time, cumulating to about seven weeks per year.

In her book, *The 30% Solution*, Lewena Bayer goes through various studies, research and analyses to show the downside of incivility and more; how it affects the organization, and how civility can increase an organization's revenue to about thirty percent more than. Impressive, isn't it?

As a leader, how do you create civility within an organization?

* Be an ideal model
* Create interactive platforms and meetings
* Teach civility among members
* Bring good and bad actions of incivility to book
* Have a periodic assessment of the company's growth and interpersonal relationship

5. BE AN IDEAL MODEL

The leader acts as a model for the organization they lead. An organization where the leader is uncivil and aggressive will reflect on the members of the organization. The same applies when you, as the leader are civil towards the people. That is why you have to adopt this humane character for yourself, in the most real way that you can.

6. CREATE INTERACTIVE PLATFORMS

If you want to manage civility with your people, you have to create platforms where people get to meet and relate. It does not have to be for professional meetings and discussions alone. Create a fun time. Organize get-togethers. That is why you have to teach. Have meetings where people can share their creative ideas with the group.

In an organization where I once worked, when there is a call for a meeting it should be pleasurable and even a delight for the workers.

1. We can share what we need to improve on, for our wellbeing and the company.
2. We keep abreast of tasks and their requirements; we are mentally prepared.
3. We get the chance to relate with people in other departments.
4. We get to taunt the managers about bonuses. And of course, we get "item 7–a takeaway".

This way, the feedback mechanism, and the interpersonal relationship remove tension. They make the people relate and speak their minds without fear for repercussions. In return, you are set on the course for productivity.

7. TEACH CIVILITY TO YOUR PEOPLE

What people don't know or see, they rarely become. That is why you have to teach people about civility. It is normal to invest in things that are capable of improving productivity, and companies should also invest incivility.

Organize workshops that talk about civility. Let the people understand that it helps them. Let them be conscious about developing this attribute as a part of their responsibilities. Sometime back, a mentor who worked at an information management company in North Carolina shared with me how he learned things that helped to improve life in his office. I asked if that was normal; learning extracurricular activities that extends the working environment from work-organized workshops. He said yes. Guess what they talked about? Yeah, it was civility!

If you want your staff to adopt it, teach it!

8. RESPECTFUL WORKPLACE POLICY

Something I would love to discuss here is about the Respectful Workplace Policy. Usually, every organization is meant to have this policy. Sadly, a few don't, have, while many have it, but are inoperative. If you lead a startup or you intend to, you should have it incorporated. It is a good thing; you will be glad you did. You know, of course, that you have to uphold the policies yourself.

Respect is quite vital among staff. Respect in a workplace is not about who is older or who has a better education or qualifications; it is learning to appreciate and value people. You should teach this to your staff. They should respect people for what they stand for and what they contribute to. If you are a leader or a manager of a group within an organization, you should teach this to your teammates. Bringing out values in people makes them lively at their functions. Respect among individuals is known to be the most effective way to make them express themselves without fear. During one of our national Association for Image Consultants International conference in Nigeria, I was speaking with one of the attendants that worked with the hall we used. Jovially, we were talking about the conditions governing securing jobs in the country. He said in the country's Pidgin English, translated "Life has dealt with most of us in the cruelest ways possible. However, for me, I think God just used this workplace to ease me of most of those life worries. Our manager treats us with importance. He does not say because I am a cleaner, I don't have a say in how things should go around the organization. Sometimes, he asks questions about how my family and I are faring. Hearing such caring words mean so much to me. Though getting cleaning jobs is easy around here, getting somewhere to work without tension is a blessing."

Before I left the venue, I asked to see the manager and I appreciated him as a human being, among my other accolades for making the atmosphere conducive for the meeting.

The *ProActive ReSolution* Workplace [6] Survey gave a statistical analysis of the survey done for about 8,000 employees and managers about the awareness and practice of the Respectful Workplace Policy within their workplace. The study found:

- 31% of respondents weren't aware of their organization's respectful workplace policies.
- Of the 69% who were aware of the policy, 58% said their organizations hadn't prepared them to respond appropriately when they were treated disrespectfully, specifically:
- 55% said their organizations had not prepared them to respond appropriately to behavior that made them feel uncomfortable.
- 58% said their organizations had not prepared them to respond appropriately when they were treated disrespectfully.
- 64% said their organizations had not prepared them to respond appropriately when they were fearful of being ridiculed or belittled.
- 32% said they were aware of 2-5 past incidents of disrespectful behavior.

9. BRING ACTIONS TO BOOK

It is both a civil and noble action to commend people for their efforts in making an organization grow. You don't have to always consider that there is going to be a cost involved. Sometimes, what people need is recognition for their efforts. You can recognize people for being the staff member of the month. You can recognize people for upholding good humanitarian actions and relationships. It is a civil thing to do.

However, it is not just that. If there is any action that violates civility within the organization, there should be a repercussion or penalty for such. The penalty does not have to be harsh. It can be having an offender publicly apologize, suspension, donate to charity. After penalties, as the leader, you can also politely (without offense) thank the offender for her service. You can meet them privately to tell them you are not pleased with their uncivil acts and you would love to see them change. However, if the penalty is expulsion, let the person understand you are not pleased by having them leave. Let them know, "however, rules are rules."

10. HAVE A PERIODIC ASSESSMENT OF HOW YOUR STAFF RELATE

The best way to know if growth is occurring is by strategically measuring it. As a leader, you can tell how people relate to you and themselves. You can notice if civility happens among your people; it cannot be hidden. You can make a personal assessment of civility by observation. You can have a personal or individual interview with some of your staff to ask about what they think of the staff-to-staff relationships, leader-to-staff, manager-to-manager relationships.

Another effective approach is by creating a form that would record what the members think of the working atmosphere, the intra-organizational relationships, and how the organization (through its representatives) relate with non-members or customers. Usually, responses that are more honest are gotten when names of are not included on the form. You can have the forms printed and filled with ink, then have them submitted to your desk or your office mail.

Here is a template you can work with.

THE CIVILITY ACADEMY

Relationship Assessment Questionnaire

1. What are the things you like about US in the past one month?

2. What are the things you would like the company to improve on?

3. Have you been treated harshly recently?

    Yes _____

    No_____

4. If yes, why?

5. Do you think the harshness was justifiable?

6. What do you think about how the manager relates to the staff?

7. Whose is/are your most admirable relationship within the organization?

8. What relationship among (which people) do you think needs to be better or improved on?

9. Is there anything you would love the organization to adopt, to make its members feel comfortable within their workstations?

EVALUATING YOUR CIVILITY

I surveyed 38 companies in Washington DC. I shared questionnaires with some office managers and Small to Medium Enterprises (SMEs). Some of these people believed civility earns disrespect, due to too much familiarity with staff. As a result, they claimed that this makes staff too complacent to work. Seems ironic, but it might be true. Therefore, a similar questionnaire was shared with the staff, within the organization of the selected managers, they seemed to slack on their duties because of the uncivil treatments they faced. In a section that read, "Do you think civility can cause lazy attitude and occasional disrespect to the manager?" About 84% of the staff responded "No," and 16% answered "Not likely," in their forms. No one responded "Yes." The answers given by the managers were only assumptions, perhaps based on a feeling of insecurity.

As a leader, your civility does matter. It is communicable, like a smile. It does not just help you; it helps your employees and teammates. The exciting thing is that it spreads beyond the workplace. When you extend your civility towards your people, they also go outside the organization to show and teach others about it. The world gets better because of you.

Now, you know what to do. You can be better. You can also have a yardstick for measuring the civility among you and your teammates.

Study your co-workers:

- Do they feel comfortable sharing their ideas with you?
- Are they free to discuss issues bothering them about what they do for you?
- Are they free to share non-offensive jokes with you, at leisure?
- When last did I let a member have a say in change?
- How often do I say "sorry" or "thank you"?
- Have I shown my appreciatation to the team recently for their contributions?
- Do I still maintain my respect while disagreeing with people?
- Have I been taking advantage of people?

If you think you are not in the best position to answer these questions to assess yourself, you can create them in a table with columns; disagree, not sure, agree and share the forms with your staff/teammates. You can also create the columns, and tell them to rate you on the scale of 1 to 5, for each question. You will have more sincere feedbacks if they do not have to put their names on the forms and all they need to do is to tick the boxes. You can make it a monthly or quarterly activity.

Evaluating your civility is part of being civil. Therefore, you are still on the right path. All you need to focus on is to re-examine and make new or better strategies about how to carry out your work.

The secret that many internationally recognized organizations have learned is that they have a workplace where diverse ideas are welcome. To join this league of greatness you have to build a workplace where organizational policy is based on civility.

CHAPTER FOUR

THE LEADER AND
THE PEOPLE

My people, my heart

I have set before me a plaque
and the watchword is the people.
there is a city i love to king
it is where the people are the light
and the leader, a shining light and record keeper.
there is a group, i love to lead,
it is a group like family;
where everyone sees his colleague his brother
and hands are held with dignity.
smiles are shared with joyfulness.
like one mighty storm, we climb heights with effortless
strides.
—Louisa Akaiso

I wrote this poem about my dream for the world's workplaces. I am still on that path. This chapter will draw lessons from Plato's words about being a leader.

THE PHILOSOPHER-KING

Plato believed that an ideal leader is one who is flexible. It is the conduct of men that lead to bad results, and what was once seen as virtues that govern their actions should be changed for new ones if disaster is the result. As long as a leader is taken from among the people from a city, it is impossible to be wholly just; he would have some flaws that are common to the people.

According to Plato, for a ruler (regarded to be the king) to be effective in his office the king must become a philosopher and the philosopher must become a king. That is, the ruler must have the mind of the people, understand their position and feeling, and then think about the best way to cater to them. This, therefore, makes the king a philosopher, and the philosopher who thinks like this is a king. An ideal ruler must be just, which is the embodiment of wisdom, courage, self-control, moderation, and justice.

At no point in time should a leader forget that they are part of the people. They are only privileged to be the first person of honor. That, however, does not separate them from the people. Decisions and re-sponsibilities should be taken from the perspective of the people.

Some people have a problem with thinking it is wrong or weak to be seen thinking about and making considerations for the people working with them. They would rather see the relationship as a leader atop, with the people under them. There is nothing wrong with seeing your staff as colleagues or co-workers. We are all humans. They work to drive productivity forward, for your group or organization. No one boasts of being a head except there is a record of accomplishment for success. No one is regarded as 'head' except there is a group of people that work with him/her to produce the track record which the 'head' stands on.

In every way, the leader should appreciate and acknowledge the best resource that the earth has to offer, which he has–the people.

Interestingly, people appreciate a leader who gets along with them, is concerned about them and communicates with them. I will not need to show a statistical analysis for that. Let us consider a simple example. Do you see your kids as inferior, or a part of the family? In the family, do you seek to be feared, or you would prefer to be loved and appreciated? Do you criticize your kids because they have nothing or little to offer the family, or you nurture them to be what you want them to be?

The family relationship is a good relationship model that can be set up in your organization. In the long run, you will realize that ruling with an 'iron fist' does not help. As explained earlier, a hand of civility extended gets the people to be open with their work, willingly committing their energy and cheerfulness, and thereby, increasing the output and performance of the organization.

The people want someone responsible and respectable. That is what a leader has to understand. An African proverb says, "He that will catch a monkey must behave like a monkey." When considering hiring new staff, many organizations look for a line in an applicant's resume that shows the applicant is willing to offer credible services for the organization while she or he also learns values useful for herself or himself, as well as personal development. It is sad that most applicants never see their workplaces as a place of personal development. They only hope for the day to be over.

Work can get cumbersome, undeniably. Some days, you feel like getting the day over with, because of your heavy workload. What about when this happens every day? What do we say when people have heavy workloads and cope with harsh office atmosphere? A leader should not lose his humanity in dealing with the people.

There was a day I went to visit a friend, John. He is an executive consultant at one of Canada's largest event management companies. I had called him earlier, to find out if he would be free for a brief chat.

John said he would be available, but he would prefer we meet in the office because of a meeting he could not afford to miss. We met within his 30 minutes official break. Afterward, he said there was going to be a game in the office and asked if I wanted to stay and watch. A game? Not many high-profile companies have games during the workday. I waited. He had a card game with his staff! They formed a big circle with six groups of about four people each. They would read from the card, throwing questions at people from other groups and record the score on the board.

I watched John and the people. He wasn't wearing his jacket, his dress shirt was rolled to the elbow and the tie loose at his collar. The top button of his shirt was undone. They all shared that moment, happily. Jokes flew around, chuckles and laughter were everywhere, each group would gather to share ideas and deliberate about what answers to produce. I saw strength and unity. I asked John before I left, "It is a good practice. Why do you do that?"

"Louisa, the people make us what we are. They are responsible for my benefits. I should be responsible for their joy. The reward is more mutual benefits for us all." He replied, offhandedly, with a grin.

Every leader should be like John, not necessarily about the game, but about being responsible for people's happiness, creating a purpose. A relationship between the leader and the people is the accessibility of civility. People emulate the conduct of their leaders.

THE LEADER'S OBLIGATION TO THE PEOPLE
Be a good conversationalist, have good listening ears.

Conversation is the empirical virtue of communication. You are the people's person. Communicate with them.

There was a woman who managed an organization in the UK. She had come from Africa, but now a resident citizen in the UK. She managed a staff of black-skin people; residents, British Africans, and African-Americans. She told me there was a lot of tension among the staff. Sometimes when she called for a meeting, she would realize only 5% of the staff contributed to the meeting. I advised her to have private conversations with the top contributors to the meeting, ask them why they think others don't talk. She did, and the result gave her insights about how she could progress. About a year later, she called me to share that the people are much freer now.

Talking with your people and offering a sympathetic ear helps a leader to help the people and the organization. If you do this already, cultivate it. If you do not, develop it. You don't have to be garrulous. Having someone to listen is healing and therapeutic. Something as simple as this is what some people need.

Be secretive with someone else's secret.

As a leader, people are bound to trust you with their secrets, either because they found you lovable and caring or because they need help. You are not to divulge their secrets to someone else, especially when they are not concerned. Don't use personal issues as case studies, unless you have their permission. I understand how free we think we are to give instances, but there are delicate matters that some people wouldn't want to be shared or to be identified with. Respect the privacy of your staff; don't share someone else's status with others except you have the permission from the subject of the discussion. Secrecy preserves dignity two ways –the owner of the secret and the one trusted with such secret.

Review the official procedures and relieve the people of excess workload.

When an organization is growing, it is bound to increase the workload. During these growth periods, the leader should review the operating processes and check if the people are getting more work than they can handle. Sometimes, they might not admit it, however, if you consider that the organization can afford help or some different procedure might work better, relieve the people of too much workload. Change the current system if need be.

Tell them, "Hey Henry, I see you are busy. Would you like to have someone help you? What do you think about installing a new operating system that would make your job better?" They will think about it and tell you if they can handle what they are doing.

Lewena Bayer asked in her book, *The 30% Solution*, "Why exactly are our workplaces so stressful?" I bet you can count the problems on your finger and toes. For me, I will say they are stressful because the leaders have allowed it to be so. The leader is the pathway to the people's good working experiences.

Invest in the people

If you have just a week to spend with a group of people as their leader, investment is one of the greatest impacts you can give them. Investment can come in different forms; look at the one that is pertinent to you and your people and incorporate it. Investment creates familiarity, and it makes the people feel indebted to you as the leader. Here is one of the ways people become grateful for working under a leader.

Invest virtues in people. The leader is meant to develop the people, either directly or by sponsoring them for things that will help them to get better and what they do for the organization. For example, if you provide skills development for a person, it becomes a part of the person, forever. If they leave your organization, they will know that they acquired that skill while they worked for you. It is one of the gains the people accrue from having to workd with you. A leader should make an impact on his people and encourage them through their personal and career development.

You can help market strategists to develop critical thinking. You can help a typist to build her skills by getting her better software. You can help send your sales rep to conferences and seminars. Share professional tips and ethics with the people, with love and respect. You don't have to bear costs personally, the organization should pay for this. What matters is that you are the author of these efforts. Develop the people. Invest in them. A healthy workplace is where the workers and the organization benefit mutually.

CHAPTER FIVE

INTEGRATING AND MANAGING CHANGE

"The only thing that is constant is change."
~Heraclitus

"To everything, there is a season, and a time to every purpose under the heaven: ...a time to break down, and a time to dance; ...a time to cast away stones and a time to gather stones together..."
~Ecclesiastes 3: 1, 3, 5

"...but time and chance happeneth to them all."
~Ecclesiastes 9:11

I consider it needed, to render these famous quotes to sensitize the mind, to how important change has always been a part of humans. I agree with the above definitions of change. I carved the definition, myself, concisely. *"Change is the changer of all things; yet, unchanging in its phenomenon."*

I have heard and seen many people feel reluctant to change. I have been in that camp many times until I made peace with myself that change is a part of life. If you think about your childhood, you could catch a whiff of nostalgia and realize your mind has teleported you back to those wonderful experiences of infancy, before the reality of adulthood hit you like a rock. Change is a part of life. It happens to everyone, and we have to live with that. Often, we resist change, not knowing it is the displacement of a more complex practice by a simple, efficient, and economic one. This truth holds for corporate bodies and organizations. Change exceeds what anyone can contain. The only way to accommodate change is to be flexible.

I understand why people resist change, which I partly discuss in this chapter and the next one. However, if you consider the trend of civilization, you will agree with me that technology makes life easier. For example, consider your vacuum cleaner compared to a broom, a washing machine, a dishwasher, a refrigerator and lots more. Did you have any problem with buying and installing these machines into your home? I doubt you did. The same principle applies to trying out new things! Embrace and appreciate change.

As a leader, the fate of your group may depend on you. One of the things expected of you is to make the right decisions at the right time. A good decision made at the wrong time is frustrating. A bad decision made at the right and wrong time can be disastrous. Hence, you should be flexible with change.

There was an information technology company

that used a facility in Washington DC. When it was starting, it had a big banner to advertise what they do. The banner got blown away by a storm, and it was not repaired for a long time. The firm has a space that it rents out to people who want to hold meetings of less than 100 people. We once used the space for an innovative discussion. The interior is quite simple but mesmerizing. The problem for the company is that people barely know they have a meeting space. There was no publicity.

Recently, another IT company came to lease a space on the ground floor of the same building. They renovated their space. The office was decorated with its name emblazoned on the top of their office. It had a reception desk, a comfortable place for visitors to sit.

The new firm's arrival came like a lightning bolt from the sky. It turned things around. I learned something; if you want to have a competitive edge, you must be flexible as much as you are innovative.

There is one story that the Pan-African entrepreneur, Strive Masiyiwa shared on his Facebook page, sometimes ago. He was in an Uber car, on his way somewhere and he was having a conversation with the driver who was a good conversationalist. They approached the subject of change and driving. The driver said times have changed and he tried as best as he could to change with them. Strive asked what would happen with the implementation of autonomous cars. The man responded that he would always find a way. He would easily change when the job changed.

What a profound statement.

A person who resists innovative change will be relegated to the trash heap time.

"The snake which cannot cast its skin has to die. As well, the minds which prevented from changing their opinions; they cease to be mind."
–Friedrich Nietzsche.

"Yam embraces change. It becomes pounded-yam Maize embraces change it turns into pap."

This is a proverbial poem about change in Yoruba land, the western part of Nigeria. The ideal meaning behind this proverb is to depict that change often evolves into something better. The same is true by the larger probability of change when it applies to things and humans.

CHANGE AND PRODUCTIVITY

"Insanity is doing the same thing over and over again and expecting a different result."
—Albert Einstein

When thinking about innovation, it is impossible to avoid the term change or variation. The competitive edge of many profit-oriented organizations is their ability to innovate. Over the years, we have seen the information technology sector incorporate innovations, beating their previous bests. The same is true for the telecommunication industry. We have witnessed so many innovations after Alexander Graham Bell's first telephone; the walkie-talkie, the cellular, the (mobile) java phones, Symbian phones, and Android phones and tablets. If innovations, which includes change, were not embraced, we would not have the improvements from which we exercise choice.

The world of marketing has become extremely competitive. People want more value for what they buy, hence, the reason for innovations to see how best to meet these new demands of the buyers creatively. Either for profit or non-profit purposes, change brings about better marketing.

EVALUATING CHANGE

In 1997 Ackerman [1], explained the types of organizational change with a holistic approach. He categorized change into three types:

Developmental change: This can be a change that was planned and prepared for. Also, it can be emergent. The purpose of this change is incremental. It focusses the improvement of skills or techniques.

Transitional change: This type of change does not happen all at once; it happens in phases. This type of change aims to lead to the desired state. It is a second order change; it can be either radical or planned.

Transformational change: It is radical. The members of the organization, the leader, mutually make the change. The change might disrupt a current structure, practices, and approaches. The members of the organization continuously learn to maintain relevance and improvement. Transformational change is a second order form of change.

Further analysis of change breaks down to how it happens, emergent or planned.

Planned change: A change is said to be planned when it is deliberate. The group to be changed has speculated what they desire, and they prepare for it.

Emergent change: An emergent change happens when people have to embrace change as it happens. There is usually little or no preparation and strategizing for this change. An emergent change might be based on the sudden change of the organization, the environment, economies, and governmental policies. A leader might be forced to decide with, or on behalf of the members of the organization very quickly.

In his book, *Developing the leader within you* [2], John Maxwell explains that change can be either evolutionary or revolutionary. Change is revolutionary when a new method from what has always been practiced is brought into place. In contrast, change is evolutionary when the current method of practice is refined or improved upon.

Either way, change is primarily to sustain an organization. Therefore, as a leader, the responsibility to bear this sustainability is on your shoulders to implement.

During change integration and management, timeliness is paramount. You have to be current with the happenings in the market. This would mean you have to listen to the news, catch the stock market highlight, read the daily papers, listen to radio programs, stream videos online, and watch out for tutorials about the trends in your industry. In a corporate organization, information is power. You don't want to lose your grip on it.

Gathering information can allow you to create a detailed, plan for first-order change, ready for implementation. Leadership comes from work.

Time is the measure of the value of change. When a change is timely, you are praised for your foresight. Your organization in return gains an edge. To meet this challenge, you can happen on change either as emergent or as a preplanned.

However, change can go sour. If a *change goes sour,* it can be a wrong change when the time is right or a right change when the time is wrong. Either of these can sweep an organization off its balance. That is why consistently seeking information means to seek relevance. In the verse of the Bible quoted at the opening of this chapter, Ecclesiastes 9:11, the author in his wisdom mentioned things that bring about change: time and chance.

A leader has to understand the opportunity found

in timeliness. However, it would be impossible to achieve this if he doesn't have the information. It is ideal to say the first step to implementing change is gathering information. As I mentioned, the civilized leader needs to be flexible and accommodating. The mind is the first place where change happens.

THE CHANGE CYCLE

To discuss change, we have to talk about the entire process from the time it was thought of to when it would happen, and new strategizing would be done again to create an upward movement.

Observation

This is a process of discovery, which usually comes by gathering information. We have discussed how a leader is meant to scout for information because it is power. Information makes you aware of the things happening in your environment. When you have gathered that information, you are to analyze it and think of the things that you currently practice. You will consider the results from your research, and how it affects your organization or may change the way you do things.

Innovation

When you have observed the trend at hand and the one to be implemented, you come to the place of innovation. Here, you make strategies and advancements. You will have books, notes, and papers where you will have your ideas and implementation processes done. You can have a prototype of the new system to be incorporated. Sometimes, you might experiment by having one group of people that work with the new process, while another group carries on with the old way. You can get feedback and adjust until you come up with the right model.

Critiquing and Proofing

Making criticism is also a part of the change process. Partial criticism is made during the observation process. You think about possible faults in the model you have designed for implementation. Critiquing times can be severe and harsh. Sometimes, you might need to bring in a visitor who also has a strength in the same process, to check the new model, and test it.

Nevertheless, criticisms during change are meant to be constructive. Criticism should provide pointers to where there are faults and how they can be improved upon to perfect the system.

An example of this stage is in the IT industry. They perform routines protocol checks. It is an attempt to see if their security system or firewalls can be broken through, from outside the organization.

A system to be implemented must be tested and trusted to stand the test against fault, lagging, and debt. Hence, this is an important part of change implementation.

Change Induction

The next step is the full implementation of change. You will have to explain to your staff about the change, orientate them and probably take them on workshops and make presentations to get them familiar with the operations and the launch.

New Strategizing

As time goes on, there would be a need for change again. You have to keep being relevant. Once an observation is made about an operating system, and there seems to be a deviation from the demand of a target audience or customer, there is the need to re-strategize and get back to the game of observation, which is where the change cycle begins.

WHY THE RIGIDITY AGAINST CHANGE?

Implementing change is not easy, neither is managing it. As a civilized leader, you understand the situation at hand and why people might not want to change. Knowing the rationale of 'rigidity against change' equips you with the ability to help people adjust to the change that is going to take place within your group, subgroup, and organization.

Here are the possible reasons why people might be rigid to change.

1. Nostalgia

Nostalgia has a way of keeping people in the past. The thought that people would miss what they like about their present position or procedures sometime in the future can make them resist change.

What to do: Make them aware that the world is changing and there is nothing anyone can do about to negate this sad reality. Let them know that you feel the same, but we all have to move ahead.

2. Insecurity:

People feel insecure about two things; a considered successful prime and the fear of being left behind.

a.) *A considered successful prime*: Usually, it is felt by a leader first, most times. When an organization is considered to be on the top of its game, above the competitors, the manager feels he has everything just right. He may begin to shun innovations which might alter the present equilibrium. If you manage an organization that depends on people as the recipient, you still have to come to the term of Adam Smith that says "humans are insatiable." You cannot maintain their interest/taste for long; soon they will change and have a new attitude or desire.

What to do: Get your mind into the game; convince yourself that there would always be a reason for the change. Get prepared ahead of time.

b.) *The fear of 'being left behind'*: The fear of losing a job because of factory automation is also an understandable reason why people may be rigid to change. Who wouldn't want to protect his job? Sometimes, there might not be a need for replacement of a person in an organization; the organization might get rid of the position altogether.

What to do: Encourage your staff to seek relevance. If it is the case that there would be a replaced by a procedure, you can offer to get a trainer for the staff rather than hiring new personnel. This is where your civility comes in. Equipping your team members with knowledge is vital so that they gain relevance as much as they serve you.

3. The cost of change
Change is expensive and draining. It requires mental effort, especially at the observation, innovation, and proofing stages. Also, the financial implication can be high. If these prices are not paid, an organization might be required to downsize. Sometimes, when people consider the cost of the change, they would think it better to hold on to the operating procedure rather than bear the financial implication that can wear them out.

For an individual, it might be the financial cost of trying to acquire new skills. Hence, the staff might be a change-resistant agent.

What to do: Get help when needed. You must have a good model for the change to be implemented. Make sure you have back up plans for your change plan, and you are prepared to gather the necessary funding for your plan. The organization would rely on you, at this critical time, to make a decision that can sustain and grow the organization. You don't have to choose to stay in the shadows, rejecting the change happening in your operating system.

Moreover, as a leader, your civility comes into play by letting your staff know what to do. Give them hints about what lies ahead of them, let them train and prepare for the future. You can let the organization bear the cost of equipping a member with knowledge, knowing it would develop both the individual and the organization. If the organization cannot bear the whole cost, you can offer to give a percentage help, to help the person. Why should you do that? Every member of on the chessboard is important. You show understanding, by not leaving anyone behind.

INCULCATING CHANGE

Change begins in the mind. The mind has to be sensitized first. If it is not, either the result can be a resistance to change, or there would be a disastrous alignment of change and time. The mind is the first area where change begins. Hence, it is where to focus on, when thinking about implementing a new process. This is true for the leader and the staff. The mind needs to be fed with information allowed to work on that information and to be convinced about the processed idea. This mind sensitization begins with you.

In change management, civility is important. Do you remember everything we have discussed about civility and people management? Good! You will need them now. If you don't, I will wait for you to quickly go over it now, before we get going. A secret about civility and change is that less resistance is exhibited when the leader is civil. We will be talking about change from the civility perspective; how others regard change can make productivity swiftly increase.

While implementing change in your organization, you need to carry your staff along. This would be after you have gone through the information and resource gathering process. When trying to carry the people along, the first thing to do is to present the situation of the organization and compare that to the ideal situation and how change is happening in sectors similar to yours. Since change begins with the heart of people, presenting the situation of the organization to the people is essential.

When you present the situation at hand and make the gravity and implication known, you get people's attention. Since many would prefer to maintain their roles within the organization, they will either suggest a change or move the change forward.

Flow with the pattern, provide a logical reason, convincing the people why the change is needed. Some staff members may have been in the organization longer than you, and they are tremendously invested in the way things are now. Some people may refer to this act as manipulation, but it is not so. It is helping the people see a reason for what is at hand and to decide about what they want. Like Plato's philosopher king, the leader sees the people as the center of the organization. The way to get people's mind into change is to bring them into the game.

When people understand the pros and cons, they will be able to offer suggestions about change! Their suggestion will be either evolutionary or revolutionary, more likely the former. When you present the matter at hand to your staff, they will suggest the possibilities of a favorable outcome, which will come with change.

UNDERSTAND WHAT ORGANIZATIONAL CHANGE IS

An organizational change can be either evolutionary or revolutionary. It depends on you, as the leader. You have to handle change carefully, thinking on behalf of everyone. It should be thought of, handled, and introduced to the people with respect. A civilized leader handles the people with respect. Hence, in the presentation of change, the respect for everyone's office and contribution is necessary.

If you are in the organization by transfer, or you are not an executive member of the organization, some people will react rudely to you. Some will, perhaps, dare you, saying you were not yet a part of the group. They don't see any problem with the current situation. To avoid such harshness and hurt, you have to let them know that you understand change affects everyone and your aim is that the organization will be improved. Organizational change considers the people and shows understanding towards them.

IDENTIFY, EXPLORE AND CHALLENGE THE SITUATION THAT REQUIRES THE CHANGE

Before you launch the change, even after observation, you have to intently look, explore, and challenge the situation that calls for the change. This way, you are sure the change is the only option needed at the time.

UNDERSTAND PEOPLE'S ATTITUDE TO CHANGE AND MANAGE YOUR CHANGE

Your first consideration of the people should be about their feelings. Understand that they are humans, and anyone is liable to being change resistant. You should manage the people based on what you expect their attitudes might be. The different reactions to change are why this section explores ways to introduce change, subtly, without losing anyone's loyalty. You will not have to do all of the work to convince many people when you understand every individual with his/her peculiar attitude. You will engage everyone by enlisting the help of others.

MOTIVATION

To get people not to resist change, you have to motivate them. Motivation should be seen in your speech and attitude. This is only possible when you have convinced yourself about what you want to pitch in your organization. I have found that motivation helps to get people to anticipate change.

My mom had this way of getting my siblings and myself to work. One day I came home from school, and I crept up to her to tell her I was tired of school and math. She asked if I was tired of school or of math. It would be a bigger problem if I hated school more than math, she said. I told her I thought it was just math. She told me that if I quit school, there was no way I would achieve my dreams. "The way to your dreams is to stand up to what it takes to get there." That was it. These were the magic words that keep me going.

Using the anticipated end of a new model of change as a means of motivating people works, it gets them to imagine what the new process would be like. Motivation also helps them to see a reason to begin the change in the first place. Motivation takes the mind off the hard work to come.

The critical point: Motivation cultivates the attitude towards action.

CHANGE SHOULD BE BENEFITTING TO INDIVIDUALS

In marketing change you should be end-oriented. People have to able to see themselves in the change to come. If they think they have no place in the new system, they will vehemently work against it. If you are presenting an organizational change, you have to be mindful of the people. They must be able to identify themselves and the benefits in it for them.

Just as you would tell a prospective customer to buy your service because of what they stand to gain, you are to also present change because of what the people would stand to gain.

GET OPEN-MINDED CHANGE INFLUENCERS AND AGENTS OF CHANGE

You need help from influencers to implement change in a mixed group which consists of people who like change and those who are resistant to it. You can create a committee of change influencers. They are those who are open to consider and embrace the change.

Such people have the following characteristics:
* Adventurous
* Innovative
* Discuss the positive outcome of change
* Research new operation procedures
* Intellectual/logical conversation

Once you can identify people with these characteristics,

you can strategically place them to influence others by engaging them in innovative discussions and the possibility of increased productivity.

WITH THE INFLUENCERS TEAM, LIST THE PROS AND CONS OF THE INTENDED SYSTEM

When you have built a team to help you with the proofing and critiquing stages, get them to list the pros and cons of the new model. You have to be factual and credible here. There is no need for pretense. It is better you have the advantages and disadvantages discussed and sorted before the implementation. When the members of the change committee are aware of this, it will be easier for them to handle.

When it is sure that the advantages surpass the disadvantages, discuss with the team how to manage the cons, minimizing any adverse effects. Do the brainstorming together. That way, each member of the team knows what to do in his or her subgroups within the organization. If everyone is part of this process, everyone will feel aware of what to do and how to manage the situation.

LET THE PEOPLE HAVE A SAY AND IMPACT

Present the change as though it is the people's choice. This is only possible when the agents and influencers have succeeded in their roles; making everyone reach a consensus of the forward motion. When the people feel a change is mutually agreed to, they commit their hearts to the development. In all you do, don't lose the focus of always making the people know that the change belongs to everyone.

Here is a list that will help when you are trying to handle a change with civility.

1. **Do we need this change now?**
2. **How best do I present the situation to the people?**
3. **How best will the change help the team members as much as the organization?**
4. **Am I carrying the team members along?**
5. **Who are my possible influencers?**
6. **What will most likely be the people's challenge and how do I handle it?**
7. **Is there a way I can help the team members to function effectively within this change?**
8. **Do we have enough information to execute the change?**
9. **Do we have all the resource it takes to implement the change?**
10. **Will the cost in no way harm the members?**

These questions are not just to be answered either as yes or as no. They need your full engagement. You might need a pen and paper, too.

CONCLUSION

It has been an exciting and fascinating discussion so far. It is a pleasure to share my insights with you. The truth is, writing this book has been enlightening to me. We have come to realize who a leader is, and the qualities of a civilized leader. Leadership is a call to work, not a title of enthronement. The purpose of power given to a person over a group of people is for service.

The leader is to be confident in himself. He is to go through a series of personal training and development periods that will sharpen his qualities to bring out the best attribute in the workplace. A leader of the people is to mold himself and the people to be better.

The productivity and achievement of goals in an organization is dependent on the persona of the leader. He is responsible for ensuring that all the organization's goals are achieved. As a result, he will have to make decisions, gather and analyze relevant information, keep contacts and maintain an equilibrium with the internal operations and external reactions to the services offered.

The people are one of the responsibilities of a leader. Because of the people, he is a man of the people. He can't hide away from people. Therefore, he has to create a civil atmosphere where they can work. He is to respect them as humans, individuals, group members and for the services they render. Investment becomes an important part of this equation that maintains the people as the primary resource of an operation.

SUMMARY

The Civilized Leader offers an insight into leadership: a leader and his people. The book explores history and factual information to show the situation that many workplaces have found themselves in. It goes further to explain the reason why some people act as they do.

This book is a manual that offers insight into civility and the flexibility of a leader. An important aspect of credibility and diplomacy is brought to light. A leader's diplomacy and flexibility should never violate his credibility.

Change management: the civility perspective should become prominent in workplaces, to let the people decide what they want, without resisting change. The leader needs to come to the place of understanding organizational change, the people, and how to affect productivity through a mutual, organizational focusing lens.

REFERENCES

CHAPTER 1

1. John Maxwell, *Developing the leader within you*, Thomas Nelson Publishers, 1993, p. 1.
2. John Maxwell, *Developing the leader within you*, Thomas Nelson Publishers, 1993, p.5.

CHAPTER 2

1. RC Sproul, *Objections Answered*, 1978.

CHAPTER 3

1. https://en.wikipedia.org/wiki/Civility "Civility, Wikipedia. Culled on 29/08/2018.
2. Merriam Webster Dictionary https://www.merri-am-webster.com/dictionary/civility. Culled on 29/08/2018.2.
3. Merriam Webster Thesaurus, Civility, https://www.merriam-webster.com/thesaurus/civility. Culled on 29/08/2018.
4. Civility Experts Inc. https://www.civilityexperts.com/ culled on 29/08/18.
5. *Harvard Business Review*, January 2013, The Price of Incivility https://hbr.org/2013/01/the-price-of-incivility. Culled on 08/18/2018.
6. The ProActive ReSolution, Respectful Work-

place Policy https://hiring.monster.com/hr/hr-best-practices/workforce-management/employee-performance-management/satisfied-employees.aspx. Culled on 27/08/2019.

CHAPTER 4

1. Civility Experts Inc. https://www.civilityexperts.com/. Culled on 29/08/18.

CHAPTER 5

1. www.jisc.ac.uk./guides/change-management/types-of-change
2. John Maxwell, *Developing the leader within you*, Thomas Nelson Publishers, 1993, p.63.